ZOO SCIENTISTS
TO THE
RESCUE

PATRICIA NEWMAN
PHOTOGRAPHS BY ANNIE CRAWLEY

M MILLBROOK PRESS · MINNEAPOLIS

FOR EVELYN, WHO GAVE ME A GENTLE NUDGE –P.N.

ZOO SCIENTISTS SHINE A LIGHT ON HOW WE CAN EFFECT POSITIVE CHANGE IN OUR WORLD. ANIMALS NEED US TO BE THEIR VOICE, I HOPE TO INSPIRE ALL WITH PASSION FOR CONSERVATION AND EDUCATION. –A.C.

My profound thanks to the following people, without whom this book would not have been possible: Meredith Bastian, Ph.D., Curator of Primates, Smithsonian's National Zoo; Jeff Baughman, Field Conservation Coordinator, Cheyenne Mountain Zoo; Rachel Santymire, Ph.D, Director, Davee Center for Epidemiology and Endocrinology, Lincoln Park Zoo; John Hughes, Wildlife Biologist, National Black-footed Ferret Conservation Center; Kimberly Fraser, Education Specialist, National Black-footed Ferret Conservation Center; Daylan Figgs, Senior Environmental Planner, City of Ft. Collins Natural Areas; Kate Rentschlar, Land Management Assistant, City of Ft. Collins Natural Areas; Kim Lengel, Vice President for Conservation and Education, Philadelphia Zoo; Jennifer Zoon, Communications Specialist, Smithsonian's National Zoo; and Erica Meyer, former Public Relations Manager, Cheyenne Mountain Zoo. Each day these dedicated people share animal conservation stories and labor against extinction. You are my heroes.

And applause for photographer, fellow conservationist, and friend Annie Crawley, who shares my passion for helping our readers care.

Millbrook Press
A division of Lerner Publishing Group, Inc.
241 First Avenue North
Minneapolis, MN 55401 USA

For reading levels and more information, look up this title at www.lernerbooks.com.

Main body text set in Adrianna 12/19. Typeface provided by Chank.

Library of Congress Cataloging-in-Publication Data

The Cataloging-in-Publication Data for *Zoo Scientists to the Rescue* is on file at the Library of Congress.
ISBN 978-1-5124-1571-1 (lib. bdg.)
ISBN 978-1-5124-5113-9 (eb pdf)

Manufactured in the United States of America
1-39929-21394-3/30/2017

CONTENTS

Xerxes is a ten-year-old male lion who lives in the African Savanna area at Seattle's Woodland Park Zoo.

THE ZOO:
A LIVING LIBRARY

In wildness is the preservation of the world.
—Henry David Thoreau

INSIDE THE ZOO, THE WILD, THE RARE, AND THE EXOTIC AWAIT. Animals and habitats you've only read about come to life. Down one path, macaws squawk in the hot, sticky air of the tropical rain forest. Down another path, hippos wallow in ponds surrounded by muddy banks. Up a steep hill, condors perch in their nests and look at the world below them.

Inside the zoo, the distance between continents shrinks. African lions roar. Asian siamangs hoot. North American alligators snap their gigantic jaws. Australian kookaburras laugh.

More than 181 million people visit zoos every year. That's more than the number of people who attend Major League Baseball, pro hockey, pro basketball, and pro football games combined. But zoos aren't just entertainment centers, they are living libraries. Zoos allow us to get close enough to animals to hear their stories. Stories in which humans often play a part—either as hero or villain.

Zoos also give scientists an up-close look at animals that are difficult to observe in the wild. These scientists use their training and a hefty dose of ingenuity to study the animals in their care. What do these animals eat? How do they reproduce? Where do they fit in their natural habitats? How do we preserve them in the wild? The answers to these questions unlock the animals' secrets.

Read on to meet three zoo scientists who are adding to our knowledge of three remarkable species. Meredith Bastian once lived among wild orangutans and now shows zoo visitors how to help these hairy apes survive. Jeff Baughman helps rescue black-footed ferrets from the brink of extinction by breeding them in the zoo and reintroducing them into the wild. And Rachel Santymire uses zoo science to give critically endangered wild black rhinos in South Africa a fighting chance.

These scientists have played important roles in their animals' stories—stories full of adventure, tragedy, and joy that unfold much like your favorite novel.

Meredith Bastian (left), Jeff Baughman (top right), and Rachel Santymire (bottom right) each work at a different US zoo. Their scientific work helps save endangered species.

FEATURED ANIMAL: Orangutan

SCIENTIFIC NAME: *Pongo abelii* (Sumatran) and *Pongo pygmaeus* (Bornean)

FEATURED SCIENTIST: Dr. Meredith Bastian

FEATURED ZOO: Smithsonian's National Zoo

ANIMAL STATUS: Critically endangered

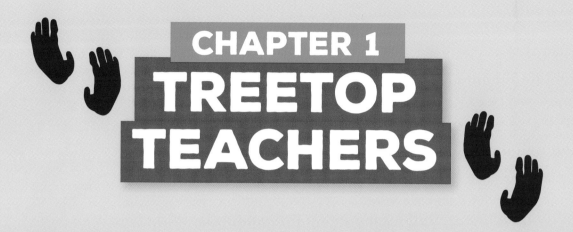

CHAPTER 1
TREETOP TEACHERS

ZOO VISITORS WHO STARE INTO BATANG'S WARM BROWN EYES SEE INTELLIGENCE. A twenty-one-year-old orangutan, she lives at the Smithsonian's National Zoo in Washington, DC. Many of the things she does might remind you of . . . well, *you!* At bedtime, she often makes a pillow and blanket for her nest of hay. And she cuddles her young son, Redd, as lovingly as you might cuddle a younger sibling or a pet.

A sign outside the orangutan enclosure at the National Zoo explains that the apes' red coloring mimics shadows in the forest's canopy. As little as 30 feet (9 meters) above the forest floor, orangutans essentially disappear, which is surprising given their bulk. Fully grown wild male orangutans can weigh up to 220 pounds (100 kilograms) and wild females can weigh up to 120 pounds (54 kg). Zoo orangutans tend to be between 50 to 100 pounds (23 to 45 kg) heavier because of their nutritious diet. Visitors who watch orangutans travel the O-Line, the zoo's overhead trail, discover that they look like kids scaling a cargo net on the playground.

Wild orangutans live in only two places in the world: the Southeast Asian islands of Sumatra and Borneo. But those populations are at risk because the number of trees on the islands shrinks every year. Farmers burn the forest to clear the land for palm oil plantations. Palm oil is a cash crop for the farmers and is a common ingredient in many everyday items, including cookies and cakes, lotions, shampoos, and toothpastes. The remaining estimated 54,000 Bornean orangutans and 14,600 Sumatran orangutans live in isolated forest fragments, where they struggle to find enough food. Sometimes they eat and nest in oil palm trees on the plantations, but when they do so, they are more likely to have contact with people and dogs that might hurt or kill them.

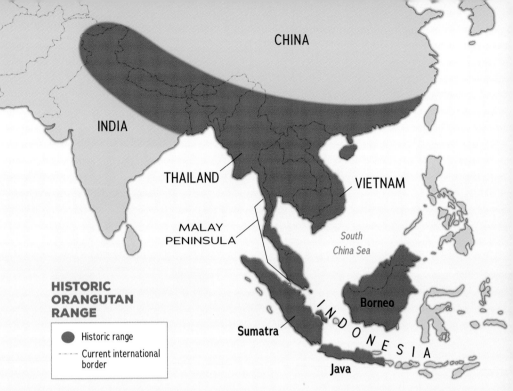

HISTORIC ORANGUTAN RANGE

● Historic range

-·-·- Current international border

CURRENT ORANGUTAN RANGE

● Sumatran orangutan range

○ Bornean orangutan range

-·-·- Current international border

IS YOUR CEREAL KILLING ORANGUTANS?

Gulp. You probably didn't know that your breakfast affects orangutans. Cereal, cookies, chips, candy, soups, doughnuts—nearly every food packaged in a box or a bag contains palm oil. Sometimes the label simply says palm oil, and sometimes it lists a complex scientific name, such as cetyl palmitate, which means the same thing. Palm oil is the most common type of vegetable oil used around the world. Most palm oil comes from huge plantations or farms in areas where humans have cut down or burned rain forests. The animals that lived in these forests either died or moved elsewhere. But thanks to the Cheyenne Mountain Zoo, the Philadelphia Zoo, the Smithsonian's National Zoo, and other conservation organizations, many manufacturers have begun to buy deforestation-free palm oil from plantations that don't destroy rain forest habitat. If you love Cheerios, the news is good. General Mills purchases palm oil from orangutan-friendly farmers. But what about your snacks, soaps, and toothpaste? Download the Cheyenne Mountain Zoo Palm Oil app for Android or Apple devices to find out if the products you buy keep orangutans safe.

The Cheyenne Mountain Zoo Palm Oil app allows users to scan a bar code and find out if the product contains palm oil from orangutan-friendly sources.

Fortunately for orangutans, friends such as Meredith Bastian are fighting for their survival. Meredith worked first at the Philadelphia Zoo in Pennsylvania before moving to the National Zoo. Both zoos hired her because of her wild perspective. She lived in the peat swamps of Borneo for seven years studying orangutans. Meredith learned how orangutans search for food, what they eat, and what threatens their existence. Her knowledge allows her to help educate both zoo visitors and the zoo workers who care for orangutans.

Meredith has been passionate about apes since she was a young child. "I grew up with the National Zoo as my home zoo," she says. "When I was eight we had to interview someone in our area of interest for a Language Arts project. I asked my mother to call the zoo." In a twist of fate, Meredith spoke with the curator of primates—the woman in the same position Meredith now holds two decades later. In graduate school, Meredith spent three months in Thailand studying gibbons. Soon after, she began studying the culture of wild orangutans in the forests of Borneo.

Meredith's research in Borneo included studying these females, who she called Wina and Wati (top). During flood season, she encountered waist-deep water (bottom), and once while building a bridge, she cut herself. She stitched up the cut using thread from her backpack.

Meredith didn't simply pitch a tent in the forest and watch orangutans. Her field study in the wild required grit and determination. Much of the Bornean forest is a humid peat swamp—paradise for orangutans but a headache for humans. In the peat swamp, dead leaves and branches do not fully decompose in the wet soil. They form a soggy peat that makes a walk through the forest an exhausting slog. In the wet season, mud, muck, and mosquitoes await. In the dry season, the peat burns like dried kindling, choking humans and animals alike with smoke.

Although she weighs only 110 pounds (50 kg) and stands just 5 feet 3 inches (1.6 m) tall, Meredith has the endurance of an ox. She and her assistants built small buildings for their base camp and hacked away jungle vines and branches for paths. They built plank boardwalks leading out of camp and several yards into the forest so they could walk above the muck to reach the orangutans faster. And they hauled food, tools, lumber, and first aid equipment to the camp by riverboat.

Meredith and her research team built this camp along the Lading River. They named it Sungai Lading (*sungai* means *river* in Indonesian).

APE OR MONKEY?

The best way to tell apes from monkeys is to examine their teeth and the relative sizes of their limbs. But those comparisons require advanced science know-how. For now, try these suggestions:

CHARACTERISTIC	MONKEYS (BABOONS, MACAQUES, COLOBUS, MARMOSETS, TAMARINS, CAPUCHINS, LANGURS AND GUENONS)	APES (GREAT APES: ORANGUTANS, GORILLAS, CHIMPANZEES, BONOBOS, AND HUMANS; LESSER APES: GIBBONS AND SIAMANGS)
External tails?	Usually yes	No (apes have tailbones, but they are not visible outside the body)
Size	Generally small to medium-sized	Generally large
Favorite sense	Vision	Vision
Create tools?	Some, yes (including capuchins and macaques)	Yes (apes solve problems with tools; orangutans are complex tool users)

This monkey is a François' langur.

This young gorilla is a type of ape.

Every morning Meredith left camp between three thirty and four thirty. She stationed herself below an orangutan's nest to be in position to observe everything that particular ape did. Sometimes Meredith traveled a few miles. Other times, she sat at the base of a single tree all day watching the ape feed. She almost always returned to camp after dark, once the orangutan had built its night nest on sturdy leafy branches.

Even as the peat swamp threw many obstacles in her way, Meredith remained committed to her research. She waded through neck-deep water, peeled leaches from her arms and legs, and battled forest fires to save her camp. During one flood season with extremely high water, the camp cook was able to fish for supper without getting out of bed! In spite of all the hardships, Meredith and her assistants logged more than three thousand hours of observation time at her study site. The data she and her colleagues gathered added new chapters to the orangutans' story and taught Meredith much more about the nature of wild orangutans than she could learn from books or scientific papers.

Meredith searching the treetops for orangutans. The machete at her waist was essential as she hacked through dense vegetation.

During Meredith's time with the red apes, she became sick with typhoid and malaria, but she never considered leaving. "It was my life and I was doing something meaningful," she says. "These animals are absolutely incredible. It's not just seeing them of course, it's also living with them in their forest." But after years in the peat swamp in various parts of Borneo, she developed a severe allergy to a family of trees that orangutans regularly eat. Her face swelled to twice its normal size, and her eyes swelled completely shut. "My whole body felt like it was being burned alive. It was pretty awful," she says. She finally left Borneo in 2010 but worried about how she could continue to be a voice for wild orangutans.

At about that time, the Philadelphia Zoo came calling. The zoo had a new mission—to integrate conservation into all aspects of its operation. Meredith's perspective was just what the zoo needed to launch this ambitious new plan. "Meredith provided the bridge between two worlds—wild and captive," says Kim Lengel,

When palm oil farmers burn Bornean forest, they destroy wild orangutan habitat.

vice president for conservation and education at the Philadelphia Zoo. "She had a foot in the field and a foot in the zoo. She inspired us to think about how to include conservation as a piece of everything we do here." Meredith educated the zoo so the zoo could educate its visitors.

For example, while living in the peat swamp, Meredith saw firsthand how orangutan habitat was destroyed to make way for palm oil plantations. The dwindling numbers of trees for food and nesting meant that competition between the apes increased, resulting in fewer chances to spend time together and learn from one another. Instead, they spent the majority of the day staying one step ahead of starvation.

To help protect wild orangutans, Meredith suggested that the Philadelphia Zoo partner with the Sumatran Orangutan Conservation Programme (SOCP). The organization's drone technology monitors changes in wild orangutan habitats. "A colleague of mine at SOCP started using human-controlled drones that fly over the forest to count orangutan nests," Meredith says. Zoo visitors learn that the drones provide more efficient, accurate, and timely nest count data for improved conservation decisions. "It's much safer [and less expensive] than what we used to do— take off from the river in an ultralight airplane that would sometimes crash," she says.

The zoo launched another program after Meredith found out that palm oil growers had burned her Bornean camp to the ground. "The forest she studied was gone, and her orangutans likely could not have outrun the fire," Kim says. "I remember her in tears. All these animals that she had lived with and come to know as individuals were probably burned to death." The zoo developed a palm oil education campaign out of respect for Meredith's lost

Visitors to the Melbourne Zoo in Australia study the palm oil exhibit to understand how to choose products that contain only orangutan-friendly palm oil.

orangutans. "Each day we probably use or eat twenty products containing palm oil," Kim says. "We wanted to change the casual visitor into someone who would take action to buy products with palm oil from growers dedicated to preserving forests rather than destroying them."

Meredith helped the zoo integrate conservation into its message in several small ways as well. For example, signs outside the Sumatran orangutan enclosure include what the ape eats, where it lives, and its conservation status. Meredith's knowledge helped zoo staff and volunteers develop updated presentations that explain the plight of critically endangered wild orangutans. And Meredith spoke with donors about supporting the zoo's efforts to save these unique red apes.

Animal care workers also benefited from Meredith's wild perspective. Her daily observations in the peat swamp meant that she knew specific details about wild orangutans' routines, such as how they care for their young, when they sleep or forage, what they eat, and how much they eat. "Meredith's information allowed us to feed the orangutans new foods," Kim says. New foods exercise different chewing muscles and stimulate foraging behaviors.

Zoo orangutans don't forage as much as wild ones do, so they need exercise to keep them healthy. Meredith helped the Philadelphia Zoo design an overhead trail system that gives

Orangutan means "person of the forest" in the Indonesian and Malay languages. Legends say orangutans are people who refused to speak because they were afraid they'd be put to work.

monkeys and apes the choice to either travel through the zoo far above the heads of visitors or to stay in their enclosures. Field data from Meredith's notebooks provided information on how far the animals can reach or jump. "I [also] interpreted for visitors and donors how the trail allowed the animals to exhibit very natural behaviors that are used by primates in the wild," she says. In a research study about the effects of the new trail, she showed that the animals spent more time exercising and had more control over where they went in the zoo than they did before the trail opened.

In 2014 Meredith moved from the Philadelphia Zoo to the National Zoo. Just as she did in Philadelphia, Meredith works behind the scenes to educate staff so the zoo can educate its visitors. "The most significant role that the National Zoo plays [in] the survival of orangutans is the increased awareness of conservation we can bring to zoo visitors through informal and formal talks and tours," Meredith says. Most of

The National Zoo built overhead trails to allow their orangutans to travel much like wild ones do.

this awareness surrounds how visitors can change their habits to buy products that use responsibly grown palm oil.

Meredith also works with zoo staff to develop new signs for the Great Ape House. Updates include new photos and graphics, new content based on Meredith's experience with orangutan habits and habitat, and information about the zoo's role in saving them in the wild.

As a field scientist, Meredith studied orangutans over several years, a long-range approach seldom used in zoos. She believes this wild perspective can add to the stories of zoo orangutans. So, Meredith and a group of colleagues launched a study of nesting behaviors to compare data from the zoo's apes to nesting data she collected in the wild. How do zoo orangutans decorate their nests? Do they nest near the orangutans in nearby enclosures, or do they choose different nest neighbors? Do they stay in the same nest night after night, or do they build a new nest each night? Meredith wants to understand

more about how zoo orangutans behave compared to wild ones.

Does Meredith miss the peat swamp and the thrill of sharing the forest with wild orangutans? Absolutely. She still has her field clothes, stained with dried peat and blood. Her field notebooks sit in a zippered black box on her office shelf. When

Meredith still has her handwritten field notes from her years spent researching orangutan behavior in Borneo.

she unzips the top, the damp earthy smell of the forest seeps out. "Fieldwork can be painful and extreme, but you don't feel that," she says. "The experience of seeing these animals in the wild is well worth it."

Yet Meredith knows that she still makes a difference for wild orangutans at the zoo. "My favorite part of my job is continuing to work with orangutans and other primates at the National Zoo," she says. "And since I live next door to the zoo, I can hear the gibbons singing in the wee hours of the morning, just as I did in the forest, which makes me happy."

Perhaps some of the kids who visit the zoo today will follow in her footsteps to become tomorrow's orangutan scientists. Because of Meredith, zoo visitors—and you—are now part of the orangutans' story.

SAVING WILDLIFE: ENGINEERING SURVIVAL

The zoo community is a tight-knit group of people dedicated to habitat conservation and saving endangered species. Many zoos around the world, including the ones mentioned in these pages, belong to the Association of Zoos and Aquariums (AZA). Meredith serves on several AZA committees, including the Orangutan Species Survival Plan. "We make decisions for the apes in all AZA zoos," she says. Decisions include which orangutan to move to which zoo and what to do if a young orangutan isn't thriving. Additionally, Meredith maintains the orangutan conservation database to record how zoos impact wild orangutans. "I give suggestions to zoos that want to become more involved in wild orangutan conservation," she says. "I'm also helping rewrite the Orangutan Animal Care Manual." Meredith's experience with wild orangutans gives zoo staff all over the world a better picture of what's most natural for the red-haired apes.

FEATURED ANIMAL: Black-footed ferret

SCIENTIFIC NAME: *Mustela nigripes*

FEATURED SCIENTIST: Jeff Baughman

FEATURED ZOO: Cheyenne Mountain Zoo

ANIMAL STATUS: Endangered

CHAPTER 2
THE COMEBACK KITS

DILLINGER CHARMS ZOO VISITORS WITH HIS MASKED FACE AND NINJA-QUICK MOVEMENTS. A sleek, wiry black-footed ferret, Dillinger can bend himself in half to navigate narrow underground burrows. He startles admirers with his explosive chatter that warns them not to get too close. And Dillinger shines as an example of how zoos rewrote the ferrets' story.

About 150 years ago, black-footed ferrets roamed the Great Plains from Canada to Mexico. The Lakota call them *pispiza itopta sapa* (black-face prairie dog) and believe they are sacred. But in the late 1800s, settlers moving westward and travelers from across the Pacific Ocean unknowingly put the ferrets in danger.

From the 1880s to the 1920s, farmers and ranchers settled the prairie. They planted crops, grazed cattle—and poisoned millions of prairie dogs. Farmers claimed the burrowing rodents tore up their fields, and ranchers said the holes endangered their cattle. What they didn't realize is that prairie dogs make up the bulk of a black-footed ferret's diet. Without enough to eat, many ferrets starved to death.

Meanwhile in another stroke of bad luck for the ferrets, rats carrying the wildlife version of bubonic plague stowed aboard ships in 1899, which docked in California, Washington, New York, Texas, Florida, Delaware, and Louisiana. Local fleas bit the plague-ridden rats, and the newly infected fleas hopped aboard squirrels, rats, and other rodents. Plague spread to the plains, where it eventually reached black-footed ferrets. Historians say that the three *p*'s contributed to the demise of black-footed ferrets: plowing, poisoning, and plague. Plowing the Great Plains reduced the black-footed ferrets' habitat. Poisoning prairie dogs killed off their food supply. And plague killed them

Kimberly Fraser with the National Black-footed Ferret Conservation Center points out a historical photo of poisoned prairie dogs.

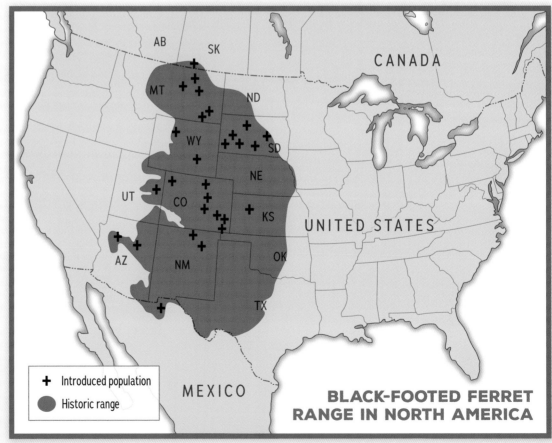

+ Introduced population

● Historic range

BLACK-FOOTED FERRET RANGE IN NORTH AMERICA

because they have no natural immunity to the virus. Scientists suspected black-footed ferrets were extinct.

Then, in 1981, a dog named Shep tussled with a wild animal on a moonless September night on a Wyoming ranch. Shep's owners, John and Lucille Hogg, suspected their dog had nabbed a porcupine. But in the morning, John found a dead weaselly-looking varmint beside Shep's water dish. He tossed the carcass into the yard.

That would have been the end of it, but Lucille was curious. She found the carcass and decided to display the unusual-looking critter in her home. John and Lucille drove to Meeteetse, the nearest town, and spoke to a taxidermist named Larry LaFranchi, an artist who stuffs and mounts the skins of animals into lifelike poses. Larry told John and Lucille that Shep had found a black-footed ferret—a species so rare scientists believed it was extinct.

Larry called wildlife biologists, who fanned out from John and Lucille's ranch and finally located about 130 black-footed ferrets. For the first time,

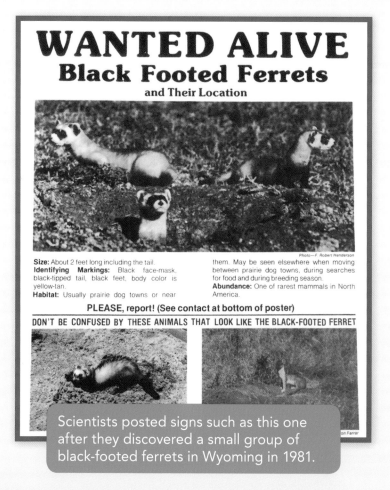

WANTED ALIVE
Black Footed Ferrets
and Their Location

Photo—F. Robert Henderson

Size: About 2 feet long including the tail.
Identifying Markings: Black face-mask, black-tipped tail, black feet, body color is yellow-tan.
Habitat: Usually prairie dog towns or near

them. May be seen elsewhere when moving between prairie dog towns, during searches for food and during breeding season.
Abundance: One of rarest mammals in North America.

PLEASE, report! (See contact at bottom of poster)

DON'T BE CONFUSED BY THESE ANIMALS THAT LOOK LIKE THE BLACK-FOOTED FERRET

Scientists posted signs such as this one after they discovered a small group of black-footed ferrets in Wyoming in 1981.

scientists could learn more about the habits of these critically endangered mammals. But in 1984, catastrophe struck again. Plague and canine distemper virus caught up with these last survivors and began killing them too. Biologists captured the remaining 18 ferrets to save them from extinction, and successfully bred them. But the ferrets' bad luck continued. Genetic tests showed that all 18 survivors descended from only 7 founders. That means that every black-footed ferret alive today also descends from one of those founders. The lack of genetic diversity makes the black-footed ferret's struggle for survival even harder.

While scientists figured out how to save the black-footed ferret from extinction, Jeff Baughman was growing up curious about all kinds of animals. "In high school, I took classes for credit at the local community college," he says. "One was . . . a zookeeping program, and I interned at the Cheyenne Mountain Zoo. That's when I realized how much zoos are doing with conservation. That really hit home." In college he majored in anthropology to better understand humans and how to solve human-wildlife conflicts. "I wanted to turn my experiences into something that would help animals in the wild," Jeff says. After graduation he returned to the zoo, where he soon had the opportunity to help breed captive black-footed ferrets and reintroduce them into the wild.

Currently housed in temporary quarters, the zoo's ferret breeding program sits atop a hill at the base of Cheyenne Mountain. Tucked into a corner immediately inside the door are Jeff's desk and computer. A blue plastic tarp separates this office space from a lab. The lab contains a large refrigerator for the black-footed ferrets' food, a sink area for diet prep, a microscope, and twenty-four jars of chemicals used to determine when the ferrets are ready to breed. A single door leads from the lab to the ferrets' living area. A sign reads, "Quiet please! Black-footed ferret breeding room. STOP. Foot bath and face mask REQUIRED for this room."

Black-footed ferrets (above) and pet ferrets aren't related. Pet ferrets descend from European polecats, while black-footed ferrets are native to North America.

COOPERATIVE CONSERVATION

Jeff Baughman plays an important role in the black-footed ferrets' recovery in North America, but he doesn't work alone. The US Fish and Wildlife Service's National Black-footed Ferret Conservation Center coordinates breeding at its site in northern Colorado and at five zoos in North America: the Cheyenne Mountain Zoo in Colorado; the Phoenix Zoo in Arizona; the Louisville Zoo in Kentucky; the Smithsonian's National Zoo in Washington, DC; and the Toronto Zoo in Ontario, Canada. The BFF Recovery Program also partners with more than fifty organizations, including federal and state governments, American Indian governments, and ranchers to return a native North American predator to its prairie habitat.

Each time Jeff moves between his office space and the lab, he steps into a bleach footbath to kill plague and canine distemper germs possibly lurking on his shoes. Remember, black-footed ferrets have no natural immunity to these diseases. And before Jeff opens the door to the ferret breeding area, he changes into scrubs and slips on a mask to further protect the ferrets from disease. "Black-footed ferrets are also susceptible to the human flu and the common cold," he says. And he doesn't want to infect the ferrets and the prairie ecosystem where they will eventually live with diseases common to other zoo animals. One tiny mistake could wipe out the zoo's entire breeding program! So the breeding facility is off-limits to zoo visitors. But Dillinger plays the role of ambassador so zookeepers can share highlights from the black-footed ferret conservation program with visitors.

In the breeding room, only one adult black-footed ferret occupies each enclosure because ferrets live alone in the wild. Built of wood and wire, the enclosures look like doll-size two-story condos. Each ferret plays and eats in the top level. "This upper enclosure somewhat mimics the prairie," Jeff says. Black plastic irrigation tubing leads to two "burrows" on the lower level. One burrow serves as a latrine, the other a sleeping area. When a female gives birth to a litter of kits, the sleeping area doubles as a nest box.

Jeff's duties change throughout the breeding season, but some of his tasks remain the same all year long. "The enclosures are disinfected every day," he says. Because ferrets are nocturnal, Jeff limits his time spent cleaning to one hour. "We want them to sleep during the day," he says. *Shhh!*

Late in the afternoon when the ferrets wake up, Jeff feeds them and provides enrichment activities, such as empty paper bags. "They like to destroy things," he says over the sound of crinkling paper as the ferrets wrestle the bags down their burrow holes. "They use the paper for nesting material, and they develop muscle tone and exploration skills for when they're released into the wild."

On the prairie, the amount of daylight cues black-footed ferrets to breed, but Jeff's ferrets live indoors. To help them behave as naturally as possible, he adjusts the amount of light in the breeding area weekly to mimic the amount of light on the prairie. As early as November, male ferrets start to feel the urge to mate, but females take a little longer.

In December, Jeff weighs the male and female ferrets. "We want to be sure they are in prime body condition," he says. Healthy ferrets tend to breed healthy kits. First, Jeff weighs an empty oblong wire box that he calls a catch device. Next, he inserts the device into the

BFF means "best friends forever," right? Not in the zoo world. *BFF* stands for black-footed ferret.

Jeff opens the nest box to weigh the black-footed ferret. The black tube leads from the nest box to the upper level of the enclosure *(left)*. A BFF is weighed in a catch device *(right)*.

nest box and the curious ferret climbs inside to investigate. Jeff locks the ferret in and weighs it inside the device. To calculate the ferret's weight, he subtracts the weight of the empty catch device from the combined weight of the ferret and the device. Throughout the procedure, Jeff is careful of his fingers. BFFs bite! After recording the weight in his log, Jeff returns the ferret to the burrow system. The whole process takes less than five minutes.

By March female ferrets begin to leave clues that they're ready to mate. "In the wild, the female black-footed ferret defecates [poops] outside her burrow to advertise that she's ready to breed. The male must find her within his huge home range. If he finds her too soon, she runs away from him. But if the time is right, they retreat to the burrow to mate."

Because zoo ferrets cannot come together naturally, Jeff relies on science to tell him the right time to introduce the potential mates. He takes skin cell samples from each female to determine if she's in estrus, or ready to mate. Jeff smears the skin cells on a glass microscope slide, dips the slide in twenty-four different chemicals, and examines it under a microscope.

First, he looks at the structure of the cells. Most ferret skin cells are roundish with a visible nucleus and appear blue or green under the microscope. When a female is ready to mate, her cell walls become jagged and the nucleus disappears. The cells also pick up an orange stain from the chemicals. Next, Jeff counts the cells to be sure 90 percent are jagged and orange. "Estrus could last up to a few months," he says, "but peak estrus is only a short while. We have to determine that peak time. If we miscalculate, either the ferrets could fight and severely injure each other or we see active breeding with no pregnancy."

The stakes are high for Jeff. If he pairs the ferrets at the wrong time, he loses a year of breeding. Each female is bred once a year for only four years so that her genes are not overrepresented. Scientists hope she'll continue to breed in the wild when she is released with her kits. Jeff's methodical temperament seems to be a perfect fit for the exacting nature of his work. "Black-footed ferrets are somewhat of a stressful species to work with," he says. "You want as many kits as possible to thrive and be returned to the wild, but there are a lot of challenges along the way to making that happen."

When Jeff determines that both partners are ready, he releases the male into the female's enclosure. If all goes well, they mate in the nesting box on the lower level. Jeff observes the process through a camera attached to the top of the nest box to be sure breeding rather than fighting takes place. "Usually one will leave

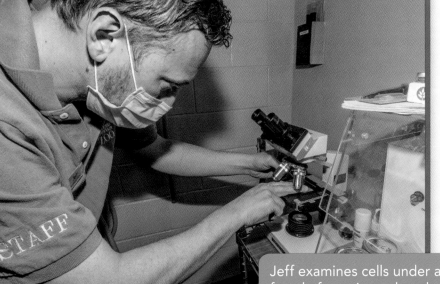

Jeff examines cells under a microscope to see if a female ferret is ready to breed. He gives each new generation of ferrets themed names. Some past themes include nuts (Pistachio and Cashew), pasta (Linguini and Fettuccini), and gangsters (Scarface and Dillinger).

the nest box when they are done—in about seventy-two hours," he says. "I close the access door to separate them and move the male back to his enclosure."

With any luck, the female will give birth exactly forty-two days later. "We've had one female give birth to nine kits, but three is average," Jeff says. At birth each kit weighs only 0.18 to 0.25 ounces (5 to 7 grams)—about the same as one US quarter. "They are blind and the size of my pinkie," Jeff says, "Their ears are tucked down tight against their heads, their eyes are closed, and they have a tiny bit of white fuzz on their pink skin. Usually I can hear tiny squeaks." During the first eight days, Jeff leaves the mother and kits alone as much as possible after performing health checks, feeding, and spot cleaning. The kits, left to their mothers' care, alternate between sleeping and nursing.

As the kits grow, they gain about 0.18 ounces (5 g) a day. Every ferret receives Jeff's undivided attention as he examines them and vaccinates them against canine distemper and plague. His

At twenty-six days old, the still-blind kits stumble around for their first raw meat. In another fourteen days, they eat their first live rodent as they begin to develop hunting skills.

passion for their survival comes through in his gentleness and his thoroughness.

Yet Jeff can't provide everything the ferrets need. It takes a group of scientists, educators, and volunteers to raise a black-footed ferret. When the kits are ninety days old, Jeff starts a new chapter in their survival story and sends them away. "It's hard to say good-bye sometimes," he says, "but I know from the beginning that [these ferrets] have a really important purpose."

Prairie dogs make up 90 percent of a BFF's diet. Ferrets must prove they are ready for release into the wild by killing a prairie dog.

All the kits and adult ferrets marked for release into the wild stop first at the National Black-footed Ferret Conservation Center's preconditioning facility—ferret boot camp. Located on the open prairie 154 miles (248 kilometers) north of the zoo, boot camp is closed to the public. Biologist John Hughes takes charge of the new recruits' training. At boot camp, the kits and breeding adults must learn three skills: navigate an underground burrow system, use the burrows as shelter, and hunt prairie dogs while in the burrows. Boot camp is the first time the ferrets have been outdoors, and they must sharpen their carnivore instincts to survive.

A mother ferret and her kits occupy one of the forty-eight outdoor wood and wire pens. Some of the grassy pens have the black plastic irrigation tubes that the ferrets grew up with in their breeding enclosures. Most have burrow systems dug by live prairie dogs. "We try to keep it as natural an experience as we can," John says.

"The next stop for these animals is the wild."

The ferrets remain at boot camp for at least thirty days. "We add a live prairie dog to the pen once a week so they can learn to kill underground," John says. So what happens to ferrets who fail to kill a prairie dog? They might be returned to the breeding program if their genes are valuable. Or they might be neutered and put on display for visitors at one of the five breeding zoos, a nature center, or a museum.

Before a ferret is released in the wild, a microchip, much like the tag your cat or dog might have, is injected under its skin. The tag doesn't transmit a ferret's location, but a special reading device helps scientists identify the ferret during checkups in the wild.

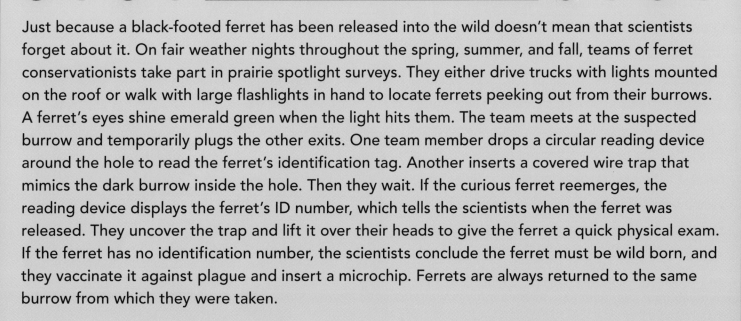

COUNTING FERRETS

Just because a black-footed ferret has been released into the wild doesn't mean that scientists forget about it. On fair weather nights throughout the spring, summer, and fall, teams of ferret conservationists take part in prairie spotlight surveys. They either drive trucks with lights mounted on the roof or walk with large flashlights in hand to locate ferrets peeking out from their burrows. A ferret's eyes shine emerald green when the light hits them. The team meets at the suspected burrow and temporarily plugs the other exits. One team member drops a circular reading device around the hole to read the ferret's identification tag. Another inserts a covered wire trap that mimics the dark burrow inside the hole. Then they wait. If the curious ferret reemerges, the reading device displays the ferret's ID number, which tells the scientists when the ferret was released. They uncover the trap and lift it over their heads to give the ferret a quick physical exam. If the ferret has no identification number, the scientists conclude the ferret must be wild born, and they vaccinate it against plague and insert a microchip. Ferrets are always returned to the same burrow from which they were taken.

Ferrets make the trip from northern Colorado to their designated release site in small pet carriers. "We usually leave around 4:00 a.m.," John says. On release day, a volunteer locates a prairie dog burrow, opens the door to the pet carrier, and tilts the carrier to encourage the black-footed ferret to scoot out. The volunteer also tosses in one last prairie dog leg as a free meal. The ferret quickly peeks at its new surroundings before scampering down the hole, on its own for the first time in its life.

"The black-footed ferret is a species in our own backyard," Jeff says. "It is an ambassador—a flagship species—for the prairie ecosystem."

The ferret's dramatic story also highlights the importance of the prairie dog—the animal that provides food and shelter to the entire habitat. The presence of black-footed ferrets reestablishes the natural food chains, which saves prairie dogs from unnecessary human slaughter. Healthy ferret populations, along with other predators, such as coyotes, swift fox, and hawks keep prairie dog numbers in balance with the needs of the ecosystem. Prairie dog burrows become homes for rattlesnakes, burrowing owls, box turtles, and tarantulas, as well as black-footed ferrets. And the burrows provide drainage from heavy rains. Without prairie dogs, the prairie would be barren. They maintain the grass by eating it or clipping it short. The short grass attracts nesting plovers and long sparrows. "Wildlife conservation is similar to playing Jenga," Jeff says. "You can remove a few pieces, but if you remove one too many, then the stack of blocks collapses."

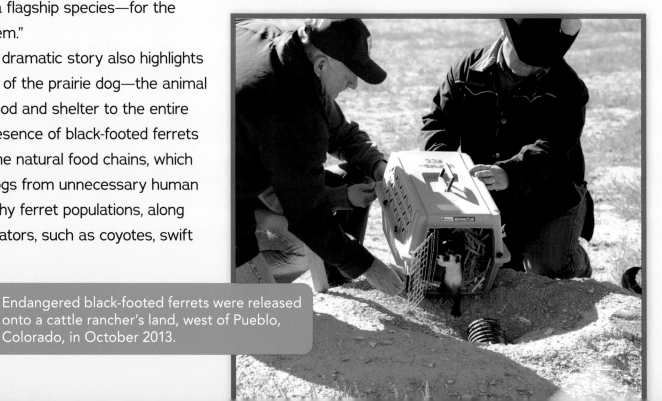

Endangered black-footed ferrets were released onto a cattle rancher's land, west of Pueblo, Colorado, in October 2013.

Occasionally Jeff will volunteer to release the kits that he helped raise. As he stands amid the thriving prairie, he's proud to know that his work at the Cheyenne Mountain Zoo plays a part in the continuation of the kits' story. "My favorite part of the job is knowing that all of the work and knowledge that goes into BFF recovery is not just for the black-footed ferret. It is knowledge gained for other species and ecosystems that are also on the brink of extinction. . . . The reward at the end is what really keeps me going."

SAVING WILDLIFE: ONLINE DATING FOR BFFS

Black-footed ferrets aren't romantic, but oddly enough, they have a dating service. Scientists call it the Species Survival Plan (SSP). Each ferret has a profile. Instead of listing the ferret's favorite color or where it went to school, the SSP records details about the ferret's family tree.

Biologist Colleen Lynch at the AZA Population Management Center is the chief matchmaker. Because only seven wild ferrets make up the gene pool for every ferret alive today, scientists struggle to maintain genetic diversity among them. Genetic diversity matters because it keeps populations healthy. The biologist examines a number of factors to choose the best male-female pairings.

Jeff is careful to follow Colleen's directions. If the male he needs doesn't already live at Cheyenne Mountain Zoo, human handlers transport him from either the National Black-footed Ferret Conservation Center or one of the four other zoo breeding programs.

Paul Marinari, a senior curator at the National Zoo in Washington, DC, manages the studbook, a record of which ferrets have mated since the beginning of the breeding program. Although the studbook used to be an actual book as the name suggests, it's now a computer database.

BFFs aren't the only species with matchmakers. The AZA oversees Species Survival Plans for orangutans, black rhinos, and many other endangered species.

FEATURED ANIMAL: Black rhinoceros

SCIENTIFIC NAME: *Diceros bicornis*

FEATURED SCIENTIST: Dr. Rachel Santymire

FEATURED ZOO: Lincoln Park Zoo

ANIMAL STATUS: Critically endangered

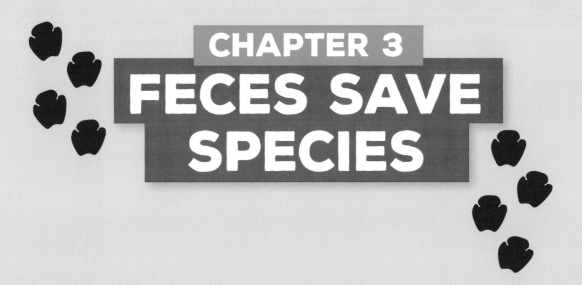

CHAPTER 3
FECES SAVE SPECIES

MAKU PATROLS HIS ENCLOSURE AT LINCOLN PARK ZOO IN THE HEART OF CHICAGO. He marks his territory by urinating on the fence separating him from his son, a black rhinoceros named King. He whines for Kapuki, King's mother, housed in a neighboring enclosure. Occasionally he rubs his horns to sharp points on a nearby wall. The wrinkles on his rough skin resemble armor plates, and his oversized head makes him look prehistoric. At 3,000 pounds (1,361 kg), he seems invincible.

But looks don't tell the whole story. Unfortunately, rhinos are no match for armed poachers, hunters who kill wild animals illegally for profit. Approximately 5,050 black rhinos remain in the world due to poaching and habitat loss. They are labeled critically endangered—one step from extinct in the wild, and only two steps from total extinction. Lincoln Park Zoo hopes to play a role in saving them.

WANTED!

Even though it's against the law, poachers shoot black rhinos for their horns. When the rhinos fall, the poachers leap from their trucks, fire up a chain saw, and lop off the rhinos' horns to sell on the black market. Most of the time, the rhinos survive this ordeal, only to die later of infection. Some people believe the horn cures cancer, relieves pain, wards off the devil, or improves their love lives. It does none of these things. The horn is made of keratin—the same stuff in our hair and nails—and consuming part of the horn has the same effects as biting your fingernails. In 2015 poachers killed an average of three black and southern white rhinos every day in South Africa. Rhino deaths are dangerously close to outnumbering births.

The poachers also pose risks for scientists. Rachel's work with the rhino research team in Addo Elephant National Park had to stop at the end of 2010. "The park staff is worried about our safety and the safety of the rhinos," she says of poachers who shoot first and ask questions later. Scientists even accidentally put rhinos at risk because poachers stake out the camera traps and stalk science vehicles labeled with signs. "We used to have rhino and elephant research magnets on our vehicles, but we had to take those off so poachers didn't track us tracking the rhinos."

Ever since Rachel Santymire graduated from George Mason University in Virginia with her PhD in environmental science and public policy, she's helped Lincoln Park Zoo manage rhinos. The zoo sent Rachel to Addo Elephant National Park in South Africa to study black rhinos in their natural habitat and learn new ways to help them. Addo Elephant National Park opened in 1931 to protect the remaining eleven elephants of the great herds that once roamed the area.

The third-largest national park in South Africa, it contains a variety of landscapes from desert to forest to thicket to grassland.

On Rachel's first trip to Addo Elephant National Park in 2007, she planned to find out how environmental pressures affected black rhinos. The park is home to hundreds of elephants, which eat many of the same plants that rhinos do. Rachel wondered if rhinos make different food choices with elephants around. And lions and hyenas live in one section of the park. Are rhinos more stressed in the presence of predators? Are they able to sleep enough? Do they breed? Rachel's data fills some gaps in the black rhinos' story. Much of this research might not have been possible without Lincoln Park Zoo's financial support and sophisticated lab resources.

Rachel worked with two fellow scientists. The trio lived in a compound of wooden garden sheds with windows, where they slept, ate, and worked in the field lab. The bathroom facilities had running water and flush toilets—positively

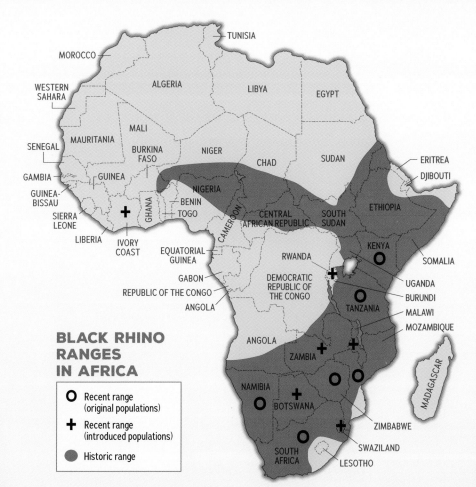

BLACK RHINO RANGES IN AFRICA

O   Recent range (original populations)

+   Recent range (introduced populations)

●   Historic range

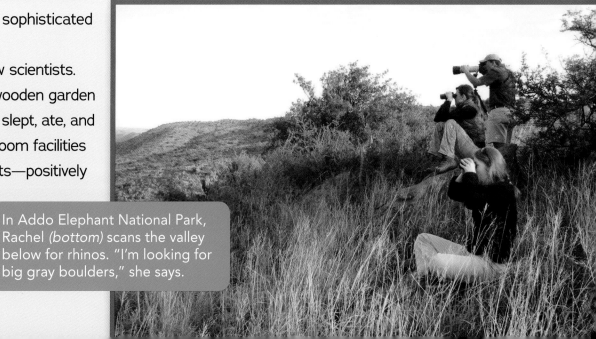

In Addo Elephant National Park, Rachel *(bottom)* scans the valley below for rhinos. "I'm looking for big gray boulders," she says.

luxurious compared to Meredith's primitive camp for studying orangutans in Borneo. The scientists traveled in a Land Rover over rough dirt roads at dawn and dusk, when rhinos are most active.

The team studied black rhinos in two of the most accessible fenced sections of Addo Elephant National Park—the Addo and the Nyathi. Twenty-one rhinos shared the Addo section with elephants, lions, hyenas, and tourists, who require roads and lodging that occupy valuable land. Because of the competition from other animals and tourists, the rhinos had less to eat. The Nyathi section supported twenty-four rhinos, but it is more remote, with fewer elephants and tourists, no predators, and more food sources.

Rhinos are notoriously hard to find in the wild. The thicket habitat screens them from view, and they work hard to avoid people. So Rachel and her team of researchers found another way to tease out clues to the black rhinos' story: rhino potty stops, also called middens.

One of Rachel's colleagues sets up a camera trap by a water hole *(top)*. At night the camera snaps a picture of a rhino *(bottom)*.

Rachel examines the feces they leave behind. "If it poops, I study it," she says. "Rhinos defecate to mark their territory. They poop and then step and scrape in it, spreading poop and their odor everywhere, saying 'This is my area.' We have the opportunity to learn about them without actually seeing them at all."

All feces contain hormones, the chemical messengers that regulate everything from digestion to reproduction. "Animals can hide certain behaviors from average observers, but they can't hide from me," Rachel says. "I can see how their bodies respond to their environments, and how that might affect their reproduction and stress levels."

To match specific piles of poop with specific rhinos, Rachel needed to know which rhino made the deposit. So the team used the middens as rhino photo booths. Motion-triggered field cameras snapped a quick succession of photos when a rhino came within range. Because Addo

Elephant National Park notches the ears of its rhinos, Rachel and her research team could identify which rhino made the pit stop. The camera also recorded the date and time the rhino stopped by. In the early morning, the team drove around collecting fresh samples. "Bacteria in the feces continually break down the hormones," Rachel says. "If you don't get the sample within twenty-four hours, it's not going to give an accurate hormone reading."

The morning after a rhino has been photographed, Rachel (left) and two colleagues at Addo Elephant National Park examine its fresh droppings.

A RHINO WHO'S WHO

Five different species of rhinoceroses live in different parts of the world. Black rhinos and white rhinos live in Africa. Javan, Sumatran, and greater one-horned rhinos live in Asia. All are in danger from poaching and habitat loss.

SPECIES	STATUS	LOCATION
Javan	Critically endangered	Located only on the western tip of Java, an island in the Southeast Asian nation of Indonesia; possibly could be wiped out by one tidal wave
White	Near threatened	Southern white rhinos in South Africa; northern white rhinos extinct in the wild (only three in captivity)
Sumatran	Critically endangered	Found only in Sumatran national parks
Black	Critically endangered	Eastern and southern Africa
Greater one-horned	Vulnerable	India and Nepal

Javan rhino

White rhino

Greater one-horned rhino

Black rhino

Sumatran rhino

At each stop, they collected feces in zippered plastic bags and labeled them with the date and the location of the midden. They stored the bags in a small refrigerator on the truck to slow the hormone breakdown until they could return to the field lab to pop the samples in the freezer. Rachel or one of the other team members would also plug the camera's digital photo card into a laptop and download the photos before resetting the camera.

Dung can spread diseases, so Rachel knew that the US government would not allow her to return home with 1,000 pounds (454 kg) of rhino poop in her suitcase. Besides, how would she keep it frozen for the twenty-one-hour flight? Rachel and her team had to find a different way to gather the hormone data that they needed and protect it on the return trip to Lincoln Park Zoo.

The trick was to separate the hormones from the feces in the field so she could leave the feces in South Africa. "The zoo is like a little laboratory," Rachel says. "We can develop field-friendly methods by taking samples from

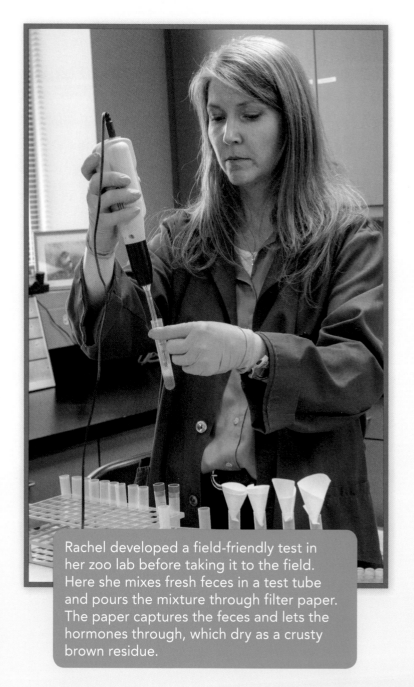

Rachel developed a field-friendly test in her zoo lab before taking it to the field. Here she mixes fresh feces in a test tube and pours the mixture through filter paper. The paper captures the feces and lets the hormones through, which dry as a crusty brown residue.

our zoo animals and trying out different ideas." Field-friendly methods are portable and easy to use. "We see what works here in the zoo lab first. That's much better than going to the field and trying to figure out why something isn't working." Especially, she says, when a lion might be stalking her every move.

Once Rachel was satisfied that her zoo-tested method worked, she brought it to Addo Elephant National Park. After morning poop patrol, Rachel and her team returned to their field lab to try it. First, she put 0.02 ounces

(0.5 g) of fresh feces in a test tube. She added alcohol, mixed the two together with a mini test tube blender, and then poured the mixture through filter paper. The liquid drained through the paper into a clean test tube. "The paper separates the liquids from the solids," Rachel says. "We no longer need the feces. We just need the alcohol that now contains the hormones." She allowed the alcohol in the tubes to evaporate, which preserved the hormones as a brown crusty residue on the sides of the tubes. "I can fit one hundred samples in a square box big enough for one cupcake in my luggage," she says. "Now I have room for presents!" The rhino team collected more than five hundred fecal samples in roughly three years.

Back in Chicago, Rachel reconstructed the samples by mixing the crusty residue with liquid. Instead of a mini blender, she used a large test tube shaker to redistribute the hormones equally throughout the liquid. Then she ran tests to determine the rhinos' hormone levels. Different hormones measure different things. For

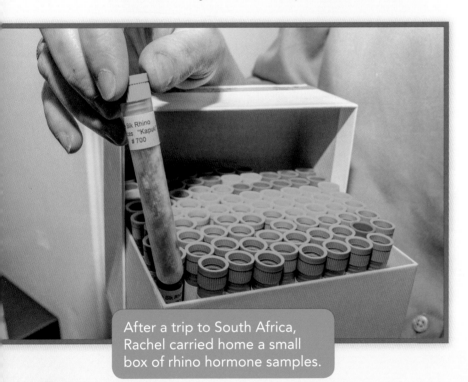

After a trip to South Africa, Rachel carried home a small box of rhino hormone samples.

instance, one hormone measures a male rhino's mating readiness. Another measures a female's readiness. Still another measures whether a female is pregnant or has recently given birth. And another measures stress.

Park managers use these data to understand what's going on with their rhinos. Rachel and her rhino team found that male black rhinos scrape their feces into long trenches to scatter it and set the boundaries of their territory. But females scrape to look for a mate—kind of like posting a profile on a dating website. If she doesn't scrape, it could mean that she's pregnant.

The rhino fecal samples told the research team that the rhinos in the busy Addo section of the park—which has more elephants, tourists, and predators—gave birth every three years. In the quieter Nyathi section, rhinos gave birth every two years. Rachel and her team concluded that tourists and predators possibly affected

Maku establishes his territory by scraping his feces.

rhino birthrates. Although it's important to connect people with nature, these studies helped park staff determine how much tourist traffic was too much for the animals. The park staff in the Addo section removed part of the fence to give rhinos more space to roam, forage, and hide from disturbances.

Lincoln Park Zoo also benefits from Rachel's research in South Africa. Much like Meredith's study of Bornean orangutans, Rachel's fieldwork on wild black rhinos helps the zoo manage its rhinos.

No longer a baby, King patrols his enclosure at Lincoln Park Zoo.

"Black rhinos can be difficult to breed in zoos," Rachel says, "and we don't have a lot of time." So she took her fecal studies in Addo Elephant National Park one step further to help the zoo's rhinos conceive a baby. In zoos, black rhinos are housed in different enclosures because they are solitary animals. Introducing a male rhino to a female rhino must be done carefully so the animals don't fight with each other. Every day from August 2011 through June 2012, the rhino keepers gathered Kapuki's and Maku's feces for Rachel, affectionately known as Dr. Poop at the zoo. Rachel tested the hormones to see if she could figure out a pattern that would tell her when the rhinos were ready to mate. But the hormones in rhino feces are already two days old once the rhino processes its food and defecates. By the time Rachel calculates the hormone levels, the ideal moment might have passed. Like Jeff with his black-footed ferrets, Rachel needed to find another way to pinpoint the perfect time to introduce two animals that preferred to be alone. She expected to find clues in Kapuki's behavior.

Rachel enlisted the help of the zookeepers—the people most familiar with the zoo's rhinos. The keepers recorded Kapuki's and Maku's behavior, such as lip curling, investigating each other's feces, shuffling feet, excitement or nervousness, aggression, and urine spraying. Scientists have already linked these behaviors and others with rhino mating. They also added the female scraping behavior that Rachel found in Addo Elephant National Park.

Rachel graphed her hormone data. "Graphing it out is so much fun," she says. "You get to see

the rhinos' response to their environment!" When she added the behavior data that the keepers had gathered, she was surprised to discover that Maku, not Kapuki, provided the clues she needed. He first became more aggressive for three to five days, probably to set up his territory around her. "Then he became the sweet rhino and would rest his chin on the bars between their enclosures," Rachel says. "That was the indication that she was receptive." At the same time, she saw that Kapuki's hormone levels were ideal for mating. Thanks to Rachel's science, zookeepers were able to bring Kapuki and Maku together at the right moment, and baby King was born in August 2013.

The zoo helps visitors understand Rachel's role in the black rhino's story. Volunteers answer questions at a specially designed Feces Save Species education station where zoo visitors of all ages can identify different Addo Elephant National Park rhinos by their ear notches, examine piles of fake poop, and study test tubes with fake hormones.

Lincoln Park Zoo visitors explore the Feces Save Species educational materials, which are based on Rachel's research.

The zoo also sponsors camps for kids interested in science. These may be kids who set up bird feeders in their backyards or fall in love with horses, as Rachel did. Or kids who volunteer at the humane society or foster dogs and cats, as Rachel did. Campers visit Rachel's lab where they weigh feces and process it much as she does in the field. The kids then graph the hormone levels and form their own conclusions. Perhaps when some of these students grow up, they will add new chapters to the black rhino's story. "I love mentoring new scientists," Rachel says. "Whether it's the kids in camp or the graduate students that work in the lab. Watching them learn and getting engaged with wildlife conservation is priceless."

Although Rachel loves what she does, she originally wanted to become a veterinarian. But she didn't get accepted to vet school when she applied. "It's sort of my sad failure in life," she says. Looking back she thinks a scientist

Rachel mentors graduate students, such as Mattina Alonge (above), who are interested in wildlife conservation.

from the National Zoo led her to research. "[He] came to one of my classes and talked about how he applied animal science to endangered species, like clouded leopards and cheetahs. And I thought, wow! If I could do that, it would be amazing."

And now she's the scientist encouraging students to follow in her footsteps.

SAVING WILDLIFE: THE RED LIST

The Red List measures biodiversity on our planet and the different pressures it faces, such as habitat loss or pollution. Maintained by the International Union for Conservation of Nature (IUCN), the goal of the list is to spur the world to act. "Unless we live within the limits set by nature, and manage our natural resources sustainably, more and more species will be driven towards extinction," says Jane Smart, the director of IUCN's Global Species Programme. "If we ignore our responsibility we will compromise our own survival." The Red List is *the* source for worldwide conservation decisions. More than twelve thousand volunteer scientists contribute data to the Red List on more than 80,000 plant and animal species worldwide. The Red List hopes to evaluate at least 160,000 species by 2020.

The Association of Zoos and Aquariums partners with IUCN because the organizations share a common goal: to preserve wildlife and wildlife habitats. They hope to work together in four specific ways:

- Introduce zoo scientists to IUCN's field scientists.
- Add the Red List status to zoo signs to show that organizations work together to save species.
- Help zoos develop conservation projects with other wildlife groups.
- Share the AZA's captive breeding know-how with field scientists.

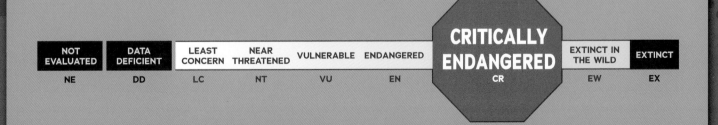

NOT EVALUATED	DATA DEFICIENT	LEAST CONCERN	NEAR THREATENED	VULNERABLE	ENDANGERED	CRITICALLY ENDANGERED	EXTINCT IN THE WILD	EXTINCT
NE	DD	LC	NT	VU	EN	CR	EW	EX

Sumatran orangutans have a large space to play, forage, and build nests at the Melbourne Zoo in Australia.

CHAPTER 4
THE REST OF THE STORY

ZOOS HAVEN'T ALWAYS CARED ABOUT CONSERVATION.

Ancient Egyptian rulers in 2500 BCE collected animals in menageries for religious ceremonies and their own private amusement. And they used the menageries to impress guests or intimidate rivals. Time passed. In the 1700s, people became curious about the similarities and differences between animals. They began to sort animals into categories to study them. More time passed. More and more people moved to cities throughout the 1800s and 1900s. Wild places disappeared under concrete. People living in urban areas began to long for a closer connection to nature. They wanted to understand the natural world. The private menageries of ancient times gave way to zoos—exotic escapes that reminded city folks of fresh air and wide-open spaces. But in this span of thousands of years, the welfare of the animals often took second place to the enjoyment of zoo visitors. For instance, small cages gave visitors a good view of gorillas or lions and were easy for zookeepers to clean, but they did not allow the animals to roam and forage as they might in the wild. Finally, in the 1980s, zoos began to recognize that they could use their animal collections to go beyond entertainment and contribute to the survival of endangered species.

The modern zoo approved by the Association of Zoos and Aquariums is more than a place for human visitors to enjoy—it is a conservation organization for wildlife and wildness. Rather than preserve just one species in an ecosystem, zoos are beginning to save entire habitats. The reintroduction of black-footed ferrets has resulted in a healthier balance for the prairie ecosystem. Working with the Sumatran Orangutan Conservation Programme preserves native orangutan habitat for the apes and everything else that shares the forest with them. And helping a South African national park make the best management decisions for black rhinos also protects the insects, birds, reptiles, amphibians, and other mammals that live there.

This 1925 photo of a gorilla at the London Zoo shows an example of an exhibit that gave visitors a good view but did not offer animals many opportunities to behave as they would in the wild.

EIGHT WAYS TO BE PART OF THE STORY

1. **CONSERVE ENERGY.** Turn off lights when you leave a room. Unplug electronics not in use. Unplug your phone or computer charger when your battery reaches full power. Every bit of energy you save helps reduce the effects of global warming, which endangers numerous species.

2. **COLLECT AND CONSERVE WATER.** When you wash fruit in the sink, catch the extra water in a bucket. Toss the last few sips of water in your glass into a bucket instead of pouring it down the drain. Place a bucket in your shower to catch water as it warms up. Use this water for potted plants or your vegetable garden.

3. **BUY SEAFOOD CAUGHT IN ECO-FRIENDLY WAYS.** Ask grocery stores and restaurants if they serve seafood that minimizes the effects of overfishing. If people in your family have smartphones, encourage them to download the Monterey Bay Aquarium's Seafood Watch app to help guide their decisions. You can also find downloadable guides on the organization's website: https://www.seafoodwatch.org /seafood-recommendations/consumer-guides.

4. **PURCHASE PRODUCTS WITH DEFORESTATION-FREE PALM OIL.** Many packaged items such as cereals, toothpastes, and shampoos likely contain palm oil. Is the palm oil from deforestation-free plantations that preserve orangutan habitats? Check the Cheyenne Mountain Zoo's Palm Oil app to be sure.

5. **VOLUNTEER FOR A BEACH CLEANUP.** Pick up debris so animals don't mistake the garbage for food.

6. **RAISE MONEY FOR ENDANGERED SPECIES.** Sponsor bake sales and car washes. Donate the money to a zoo or conservation organization.

7. **SPEND TIME AT A ZOO OR NATURE CAMP TO LEARN ABOUT THE ROLES DIFFERENT SPECIES PLAY IN THEIR ECOSYSTEMS.** Understand what would happen if some of these animals were no longer around.

8. **PLAY IN NATURE.** Discover what you love about the outdoors. Channel that love to helping wildlife stay alive.

Zoos will always have critics who say that wild animals should live in the wild rather than enclosed spaces. And most zoo workers would agree with them. But zoos provide a level of access to wild animals that scientists—and you—cannot get anywhere else. Black-footed ferrets can breed in a controlled environment until their numbers grow in the wild. Visitors can stare into the eyes of an orangutan and make the connection between these red apes and the cereals on grocery store shelves. And perhaps zoos can help the black rhinos currently in captivity breed successfully to increase their numbers in the world.

Remember the 181 million people who visit zoos every year? Every one of those people represents an opportunity for zoos. An opportunity to tell a story that helps people make stronger connections to nature. An opportunity to encourage people to consider their role in conservation problems. And an opportunity to encourage them to become part of the solution.

Zoo scientists and zookeepers care for animals and look out for their well-being over the course of many years.

You know a great story has a compelling character to root for and care about. Exotic animals are the main characters in zoo stories. Meredith, Jeff, Rachel, and hundreds more zoo scientists around the world weave their knowledge of wildlife into tales that help us better understand these animals and encourage us to care. Caring is key because we protect what we love.

Every great story has unexpected twists and turns. Zoo scientists use research to make sense of the animals' stories. "Wild is what's natural," Rachel says, as she fits together pieces of the rhino's biology with its behavior and what's happening in its environment. This more complete story allows park managers to make better decisions for the health of their rhinos. And understanding wild rhinos helps Rachel care for those at Lincoln Park Zoo. "Zoos are constantly adapting their management," she says, because animals reveal their stories slowly and over time.

Every great story has a captivating conflict that keeps you turning pages. Each year Jeff

Twobit is no longer part of the breeding program. She lives at the Fort Collins Museum of Discovery in Colorado to educate visitors about black-footed ferrets.

battles plague and the lack of genetic diversity that threaten the survival of the black-footed ferrets in his care. He remembers that black-footed ferrets have already fought off extinction once. He wants to give his black-footed ferrets the happy ending they deserve. "My goal is to work myself out of a job," he says.

And every great story changes your life in some way. Remember how the Philadelphia Zoo refocused its mission to emphasize conservation? Zoo stories encourage you to set goals for an eco-friendly life. Start simply.

Take walks to appreciate nature. Stop to investigate holes in trees, tracks on the ground, and the sounds you hear. Ask questions. Read about nature. Visit zoos, aquariums, nature centers, and rehabilitation centers to appreciate the huge variety of species on our planet. Look for a local endangered species that needs your help.

Consider the stuff your family buys. Be aware that with every purchase, you have the chance to affect change. For example, buy fish caught with eco-friendly methods, deforestation-free palm oil, and fruits and vegetables grown without pesticides. Buy shampoos, soaps, and toothpastes free from plastic microbeads that contaminate our waterways and harm animals. And carry purchases home in reusable shopping bags rather than single-use plastic bags that can harm wildlife.

But why stop there? You can be the next Meredith, Jeff, or Rachel. "We really need kids

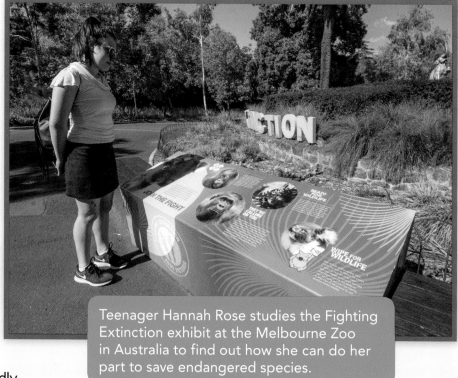

Teenager Hannah Rose studies the Fighting Extinction exhibit at the Melbourne Zoo in Australia to find out how she can do her part to save endangered species.

to follow in our footsteps," Rachel says. Start with the suggestions in this chapter, and then study biology, genetics, and ecology in college as they did. Go to graduate school for an advanced degree. Or volunteer at a zoo or a nature preserve. The stories of endangered animals are still unfolding, and you can help shape the outcome. You too can lend your voice and mind to stopping the extinction of wildlife.

SAVING WILDLIFE: THE FROZEN ZOO

The zoo world's new focus on habitat conservation also preserves biodiversity—the huge variety of animals and plants that share the planet with us. But what if the animals in an ecosystem are so endangered that they never bounce back? When one piece of an ecosystem is threatened by habitat destruction, pollution, or climate change, the entire ecosystem is threatened. Zoos need a plan B.

Plan B is a biobank, an insurance policy against the catastrophic loss of a species. The San Diego Zoo has the largest and most diverse biobank in the world. Male sperm, female eggs and, in some cases, fertilized embryos from nearly one thousand species have been cryopreserved in liquid nitrogen at -321°F (-196°C).

A biobank contributed to the success of black-footed ferret captive breeding. When a small population of ferrets was rediscovered in 1981, scientists had the foresight to freeze sperm samples from the surviving males. Scarface, one of these original ferrets, donated sperm twenty years after his death to sire Dillinger! "Because we are working with only seven founding ferrets, we can never increase genetic diversity," says biologist John Hughes with the National Black-footed Ferret Conservation Center. But by using frozen sperm, scientists can reintroduce genes that otherwise would have been lost over time.

SOURCE NOTES

5 Henry David Thoreau, "Walking," Thoreau Reader, accessed February 20, 2017, http://thoreau.eserver.org/walking2.html.

12 Meredith Bastian (curator, primates, National Zoological Park), interview by e-mail with the author, June 10, 2016.

16 Bastian, interview with the author, September 30, 2015.

16 Kim Lengel (vice president for conservation and education, Philadelphia Zoo), interview with the author, December 18, 2015.

17 Bastian, interview with the author, December 1, 2015.

17 Lengel, interview.

18 Ibid.

18 Ibid.

19 Bastian, interview, September 30, 2015.

19 Bastian, e-mail interview, June 10, 2016.

21 Bastian, interview, September 30, 2015.

21 Bastian, e-mail interview, June 10, 2016.

21 Bastian, interview, September 30, 2015.

26 Jeff Baughman (field conservation coordinator, Cheyenne Mountain Zoo), interview with the author, March 23, 2016.

26 Ibid.

27 Ibid.

28 Ibid.

28 Ibid.

28 Ibid.

28 Ibid.

29 Ibid.

30 Ibid.

30 Ibid.

30–31 Ibid.

31 Ibid.

31 Ibid.

32–33 John Hughes (biologist, USFWS), interview with the author, March 25, 2016.

33 Ibid.

34 Ibid.

34 Baughman, interview, March 23, 2016.

34 Ibid.

34 Baughman, interview by e-mail with the author, June 26, 2016.

35 Ibid.

38 Rachel Santymire (director, Davee Center for Epidemiology and Endocrinology, Lincoln Park Zoo), interview with the author, April 24–25, 2016.

39 Ibid.

41 Ibid.

41 Ibid.

41 Ibid.

43–44 Ibid.

44 Ibid.

44 Santymire, interview with the author, January 14, 2014.

46 Santymire, interview, April 24–25, 2016.

47 Ibid.

47 Santymire, e-mail to the author, February 13, 2017.

48 Santymire, interview, April 24–25, 2016.

48 Ibid.

49 "The IUCN Red List of Threatened Species," brochure, accessed March 10, 2017, https://www.iucn.org/sites/dev/files/import/downloads/iucn_brochure_low_res.pdf.

55 Santymire, interview, April 24–25, 2016.

55 Baughman, interview, March 23, 2016.

56 Santymire, interview by e-mail with the author, June 21, 2016.

57 Hughes, interview.

This baby orangutan lives at the Cheyenne Mountain Zoo.

GLOSSARY

biodiversity: the variety of life on our planet or in a specific ecosystem

conservation: the preservation, protection, or restoration of wildlife, a habitat, or an ecosystem

ecology: the science that studies the relationships of living things to their environment

ecosystem: a group of organisms that share a habitat

endangered: at risk, usually of extinction

estrus: the point in a female animal's reproductive cycle when she is capable of becoming pregnant

forest fragment: a relatively small, isolated patch of forest that remains after part of the original forest is destroyed

genetic diversity: a variety of genes within an animal population. The greater the genetic diversity, the more change a species can tolerate.

genetics: the science of how genes control traits in animals and plants

habitat: the natural home of a plant or animal

immunity: being able to resist disease

predator: an animal that hunts and kills other animals for food

prey: an animal hunted and killed for food

primates: the scientific group of animals that includes human and nonhuman apes, monkeys, lemurs, lorises, and tarsiers

species: a group of related animals that can produce young

sperm: a male reproductive cell that joins with the female egg to produce young

studbook: the official record of wild animals bred in captivity

SELECTED BIBLIOGRAPHY

Bastian, Meredith (curator, primates, National Zoological Park). Interviews by e-mail with the author, December 18, 2015, and June 10, 2016.

———. Interviews with the author, September 30 and December 1, 2015.

Bastian, Meredith L., Maria A. van Noordwijk, and Carel P. van Schaik. "Innovative Behaviors in Wild Bornean Orangutans Revealed by Targeted Population Comparison." *Behaviour* 149, no. 3 (2012): 275–297.

Bastian, Meredith L., Nicole Zweifel, Erin R. Vogel, Serge A. Wich, and Carel P. van Schaik. "Diet Traditions in Wild Orangutans." *American Journal of Physical Anthropology* 143, no. 2 (October 2010): 175–187.

Baughman, Jeff (field conservation coordinator, Cheyenne Mountain Zoo). Interview by e-mail with the author, June 26, 2016.

———. Interview with the author, March 23, 2016.

Figgs, Daylan, and Kate Rentschlar (program manager and land management assistant, respectively, City of Fort Collins, CO). Interview with the author, March 24, 2016.

Fraser, Kimberly (outreach coordinator, National Black-footed Ferret Conservation Center). Interview with the author, March 24–25, 2016.

Hughes, John (biologist, USFWS). Interview with the author, March 25, 2016.

Lengel, Kim (vice president for conservation and education, Philadelphia Zoo). Interview with the author, December 18, 2015.

Santymire, Rachel (director, Davee Center for Epidemiology and Endocrinology). Interview by e-mail with the author, June 21, 2016.

———. "Implementing the Use of a Biobank in the Endangered Black-Footed Ferret (*Mustela nigripes*)." *Reproduction, Fertility and Development* 28, no. 8 (March 9, 2016): 1097–1104.

———. Interviews with the author, January 14, 2014, and April 24–25, 2016.

Santymire, Rachel, Sabrina Misek, Jill Gossett, Mark Kamhout, Erik Chatroop, and Michelle Rafacz. "Male Behaviours Signal the Female's Reproductive State in a Pair of Black Rhinoceros Housed at Lincoln Park Zoo." *Journal of Zoo and Aquarium Research* 4, no. 1 (2016): 30–37.

MORE CONSERVATION STORIES

BOOKS

Newman, Patricia. *Plastic, Ahoy! Investigating the Great Pacific Garbage Patch*. Minneapolis: Millbrook Press, 2014.
Journey into the open ocean to explore the Great Pacific Garbage Patch with three female scientists. Find out how plastic is harming marine life and what we can do about it.

Newman, Patricia. *Sea Otter Heroes: The Predators That Saved an Ecosystem*. Minneapolis: Millbrook Press, 2017.
Scientist Brent Hughes makes a startling new discovery about how endangered sea otters protect sea grass in this story about the important role predators play in the balance of an ecosystem.

Schrefer, Eliot. *Endangered*. New York: Scholastic, 2012.
This fictional story follows Sophie's struggle to save Otto, a bonobo, in the war-torn Democratic Republic of the Congo. This is the first book in Eliot Schrefer's four-book series on endangered apes.

Yolen, Jane. *The Stranded Whale*. Somerville, MA: Candlewick, 2015.
In this fictional story, Sally and her brothers try to save a whale stranded on a beach in Maine.

Young, Karen Romano. *Mission: Sea Turtle Rescue*. Washington, DC: National Geographic Kids, 2015.
Check out this up-close look at sea turtles, the challenges they face, and how scientists are working to help them. Animal lovers will appreciate the advice on how to advocate for these fascinating creatures.

WEBSITES

Annie Crawley's Video Channel
https://www.youtube.com/user/AnnieCrawley
Visit photographer Annie Crawley's YouTube channel for a behind-the-scenes look at research for the book.

Association of Zoos & Aquariums—Find a Zoo or Aquarium
https://www.aza.org/find-a-zoo-or-aquarium
Search for an AZA zoo or aquarium near you!

Battleground: Rhino Wars
http://www.animalplanet.com/tv-shows/battleground-rhino-wars/
View a series of short Animal Planet video clips about a group of former Navy SEALs who use their operational skills to combat poachers in South Africa.

Black-Footed Ferret Connections
http://blackfootedferret.org/
The website for the National Black-footed Ferret Conservation Center includes up-to-date information as well as photos and live webcam feeds of the black-footed ferret habitat at the Fort Collins Museum of Discovery in Fort Collins, CO.

Black-Footed Ferrets
http://video.nationalgeographic.com/video/ferret_black_footed?source=relatedvideo
Follow a team of scientists from the World Wildlife Fund as they give physical exams to a colony of black-footed ferrets in South Dakota.

This Malayan tiger lives at the Woodland Park Zoo.

The IUCN Red List: A Barometer of Life
https://www.youtube.com/watch?v=VukyqMajAOU
Watch this short video to find out how scientists and wildlife specialists use the IUCN Red List.

Philadelphia Zoo's Unless Project
http://www.philadelphiazoo.org/Save-Wildlife/Join-the-UNLESS-Campaign/UNLESS-Project.htm
Get more information about palm oil, and write to snack food companies to urge them to save orangutan habitat by switching to deforestation-free palm oil.

Sumatran Orangutan Conservation Programme
http://www.sumatranorangutan.org/
Meredith Bastian's colleagues established this program to save critically endangered Sumatran orangutans with improved law enforcement, public education, habitat protections, and research.

Sustainable Palm Oil Shopping Guide App
http://www.cmzoo.org/index.php/conservation-matters/palm-oil-crisis/
Download the Cheyenne Mountain Zoo's app to your tablet or smartphone to help you and your family buy products with deforestation-free palm oil.

Woodland Park Zoo
http://www.zoo.org/conservation
The motto of the Woodland Park Zoo in Seattle, Washington, is "We need nature, and nature needs us to take action now." This page shares the zoo's strategies for promoting conservation.

Zoos Victoria
https://www.zoo.org.au/fighting-extinction
Find out what a group of Australian zoos is doing to promote conservation and fight extinction.

INDEX

Additional images are used with the permission of: © Laura Westlund/Independent Picture Service, pp. 10 (both), 24 (bottom), 37 (top), 49; © Independent Picture Service, p. 11; Courtesy of Meredith Bastian, Ph.D, pp. 12 (top) (bottom), 13, 15, 16; Mehgan Murphy, Smithsonian's National Zoo, p. 19 (top); US Fish and Wildlife Service, pp. 31, 34; Courtesy of Rachel Santymire, Ph.D, pp. 40 (top) (bottom), 41; Heather Angel/Natural Visions/Alamy Stock Photo, p. 42 (bottom right); Brian Gibbs/Alamy Stock Photo, p. 42 (bottom left); Al Pidgen/Imagine Images/Alamy Stock Photo, p. 42 (top); © RyersonClark/E+/Getty Images, p. 42 (middle); The Granger Collection, New York, p. 52; ZUMA Press, Inc./Alamy Stock Photo, p. 57.